AN ELEPHANT NEVER FORGETS...

Unfortunately I Do

A

Website: _____

Username: _____

Password: _____

Notes: _____

_____

Website: _____

Username: _____

Password: _____

Notes: _____

_____

Website: _____

Username: _____

Password: _____

Notes: _____

_____

Website: _____

Username: _____

Password: _____

Notes: _____

_____

Website: _____

Username: _____

Password: _____

Notes: _____

_____

Website: _____

Username: _____

Password: _____

Notes: _____

_____

A

Website: _____

Username: _____

Password: _____

Notes: _____

_____

Website: _____

Username: _____

Password: _____

Notes: _____

_____

Website: _____

Username: _____

Password: _____

Notes: _____

_____

A

Website: _____

Username: _____

Password: _____

Notes: _____

_____

Website: _____

Username: _____

Password: _____

Notes: _____

_____

Website: _____

Username: _____

Password: _____

Notes: _____

_____

B

Website: _____

Username: _____

Password: _____

Notes: _____

_____

Website: _____

Username: _____

Password: _____

Notes: _____

_____

Website: _____

Username: _____

Password: _____

Notes: _____

_____

B

Website: _____

Username: _____

Password: _____

Notes: _____

_____

Website: _____

Username: _____

Password: _____

Notes: _____

_____

Website: _____

Username: _____

Password: _____

Notes: _____

_____

Website: _____

Username: _____

Password: _____

Notes: _____

_____

Website: _____

Username: _____

Password: _____

Notes: _____

_____

Website: _____

Username: _____

Password: _____

Notes: _____

_____

Website: _____

Username: _____

Password: _____

Notes: _____

_____

Website: _____

Username: _____

Password: _____

Notes: _____

_____

Website: _____

Username: _____

Password: _____

Notes: _____

_____

Website: _____

Username: _____

Password: _____

Notes:_____

_____

Website: _____

Username: _____

Password: _____

Notes:_____

_____

Website: _____

Username: _____

Password: _____

Notes:_____

_____

Website: _____

Username: _____

Password: _____

Notes:_____

_____

Website: _____

Username: _____

Password: _____

Notes:_____

_____

Website: _____

Username: _____

Password: _____

Notes:_____

_____

D

Website: _____
Username: _____
Password: _____
Notes: _____
_____

Website: _____
Username: _____
Password: _____
Notes: _____
_____

Website: _____
Username: _____
Password: _____
Notes: _____
_____

Website: _____

Username: _____

Password: _____

Notes: _____

_____

Website: _____

Username: _____

Password: _____

Notes: _____

_____

Website: _____

Username: _____

Password: _____

Notes: _____

_____

D

Website: _____

Username: _____

Password: _____

Notes:_____

_____

Website: _____

Username: _____

Password: _____

Notes:_____

_____

Website: _____

Username: _____

Password: _____

Notes:_____

_____

Website: _____

Username: _____

Password: _____

Notes: _____

_____

Website: _____

Username: _____

Password: _____

Notes: _____

_____

Website: _____

Username: _____

Password: _____

Notes: _____

_____

E

Website: _____
Username: _____
Password: _____
Notes:_____
_____

Website: _____
Username: _____
Password: _____
Notes:_____
_____

Website: _____
Username: _____
Password: _____
Notes:_____
_____

Website: _____

Username: _____

Password: _____

Notes: _____

_____

Website: _____

Username: _____

Password: _____

Notes: _____

_____

Website: _____

Username: _____

Password: _____

Notes: _____

_____

E

Website: _____
Username: _____
Password: _____
Notes: _____

_____

Website: _____
Username: _____
Password: _____
Notes: _____

_____

Website: _____
Username: _____
Password: _____
Notes: _____

_____

Website: _____

Username: _____

Password: _____

Notes: _____

_____

Website: _____

Username: _____

Password: _____

Notes: _____

_____

Website: _____

Username: _____

Password: _____

Notes: _____

_____

Website: _____

Username: _____

Password: _____

Notes: _____

_____

Website: _____

Username: _____

Password: _____

Notes: _____

_____

Website: _____

Username: _____

Password: _____

Notes: _____

_____

Website: _____

Username: _____

Password: _____

Notes: _____

_____

Website: _____

Username: _____

Password: _____

Notes: _____

_____

Website: _____

Username: _____

Password: _____

Notes: _____

_____

Website: _____

Username: _____

Password: _____

Notes: _____

_____

Website: _____

Username: _____

Password: _____

Notes: _____

_____

Website: _____

Username: _____

Password: _____

Notes: _____

_____

Website: _____
Username: _____
Password: _____
Notes: _____
_____

Website: _____
Username: _____
Password: _____
Notes: _____
_____

Website: _____
Username: _____
Password: _____
Notes: _____
_____

G

Website: _____
Username: _____
Password: _____
Notes: _____
_____

Website: _____
Username: _____
Password: _____
Notes: _____
_____

Website: _____
Username: _____
Password: _____
Notes: _____
_____

Website: _____

Username: _____

Password: _____

Notes: _____

_____

Website: _____

Username: _____

Password: _____

Notes: _____

_____

Website: _____

Username: _____

Password: _____

Notes: _____

_____

G

Website: _____

Username: _____

Password: _____

Notes: _____

_____

Website: _____

Username: _____

Password: _____

Notes: _____

_____

Website: _____

Username: _____

Password: _____

Notes: _____

_____

Website: _____

Username: _____

Password: _____

Notes: _____

_____

Website: _____

Username: _____

Password: _____

Notes: _____

_____

Website: _____

Username: _____

Password: _____

Notes: _____

_____

H

Website: _____

Username: _____

Password: _____

Notes: _____

_____

Website: _____

Username: _____

Password: _____

Notes: _____

_____

Website: _____

Username: _____

Password: _____

Notes: _____

_____

H

Website: _____
Username: _____
Password: _____
Notes: _____
_____

Website: _____
Username: _____
Password: _____
Notes: _____
_____

Website: _____
Username: _____
Password: _____
Notes: _____
_____

Website: _____

Username: _____

Password: _____

Notes: _____

_____

Website: _____

Username: _____

Password: _____

Notes: _____

_____

Website: _____

Username: _____

Password: _____

Notes: _____

_____

Website: _____

Username: _____

Password: _____

Notes: _____

_____

Website: _____

Username: _____

Password: _____

Notes: _____

_____

Website: _____

Username: _____

Password: _____

Notes: _____

_____

Website: _____

Username: _____

Password: _____

Notes: _____

_____

Website: _____

Username: _____

Password: _____

Notes: _____

_____

Website: _____

Username: _____

Password: _____

Notes: _____

_____

Website: _____

Username: _____

Password: _____

Notes: _____

_____

Website: _____

Username: _____

Password: _____

Notes: _____

_____

Website: _____

Username: _____

Password: _____

Notes: _____

_____

Website: _____

Username: _____

Password: _____

Notes: _____

_____

Website: _____

Username: _____

Password: _____

Notes: _____

_____

Website: _____

Username: _____

Password: _____

Notes: _____

_____

Website: _____

Username: _____

Password: _____

Notes:_____

_____

Website: _____

Username: _____

Password: _____

Notes:_____

_____

Website: _____

Username: _____

Password: _____

Notes:_____

_____

J

Website: _____

Username: _____

Password: _____

Notes:_____

_____

Website: _____

Username: _____

Password: _____

Notes:_____

_____

Website: _____

Username: _____

Password: _____

Notes:_____

_____

Website: _____

Username: _____

Password: _____

Notes: _____

_____

Website: _____

Username: _____

Password: _____

Notes: _____

_____

Website: _____

Username: _____

Password: _____

Notes: _____

_____

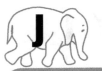

Website: _____

Username: _____

Password: _____

Notes: _____

_____

Website: _____

Username: _____

Password: _____

Notes: _____

_____

Website: _____

Username: _____

Password: _____

Notes: _____

_____

Website: _____

Username: _____

Password: _____

Notes: _____

_____

Website: _____

Username: _____

Password: _____

Notes: _____

_____

Website: _____

Username: _____

Password: _____

Notes: _____

_____

Website: _____

Username: _____

Password: _____

Notes: _____

_____

Website: _____

Username: _____

Password: _____

Notes: _____

_____

Website: _____

Username: _____

Password: _____

Notes: _____

_____

Website: _____

Username: _____

Password: _____

Notes: _____

_____

Website: _____

Username: _____

Password: _____

Notes: _____

_____

Website: _____

Username: _____

Password: _____

Notes: _____

_____

K

Website: _____
Username: _____
Password: _____
Notes: _____
_____

Website: _____
Username: _____
Password: _____
Notes: _____
_____

Website: _____
Username: _____
Password: _____
Notes: _____
_____

Website: _____

Username: _____

Password: _____

Notes: _____

_____

Website: _____

Username: _____

Password: _____

Notes: _____

_____

Website: _____

Username: _____

Password: _____

Notes: _____

_____

L

Website: _____

Username: _____

Password: _____

Notes: _____

_____

Website: _____

Username: _____

Password: _____

Notes: _____

_____

Website: _____

Username: _____

Password: _____

Notes: _____

_____

Website: _____

Username: _____

Password: _____

Notes: _____

_____

Website: _____

Username: _____

Password: _____

Notes: _____

_____

Website: _____

Username: _____

Password: _____

Notes: _____

_____

L

Website: _____
Username: _____
Password: _____
Notes: _____

_____

Website: _____
Username: _____
Password: _____
Notes: _____

_____

Website: _____
Username: _____
Password: _____
Notes: _____

_____

Website: _____

Username: _____

Password: _____

Notes:_____

_____

Website: _____

Username: _____

Password: _____

Notes:_____

_____

Website: _____

Username: _____

Password: _____

Notes:_____

_____

M

Website: _____

Username: _____

Password: _____

Notes: _____

_____

Website: _____

Username: _____

Password: _____

Notes: _____

_____

Website: _____

Username: _____

Password: _____

Notes: _____

_____

Website: _____
Username: _____
Password: _____
Notes: _____
_____

Website: _____
Username: _____
Password: _____
Notes: _____
_____

Website: _____
Username: _____
Password: _____
Notes: _____
_____

M

Website: _____

Username: _____

Password: _____

Notes: _____

_____

Website: _____

Username: _____

Password: _____

Notes: _____

_____

Website: _____

Username: _____

Password: _____

Notes: _____

_____

Website: _____

Username: _____

Password: _____

Notes: _____

_____

Website: _____

Username: _____

Password: _____

Notes: _____

_____

Website: _____

Username: _____

Password: _____

Notes: _____

_____

Website: _____

Username: _____

Password: _____

Notes: _____

_____

Website: _____

Username: _____

Password: _____

Notes: _____

_____

Website: _____

Username: _____

Password: _____

Notes: _____

_____

Website: _____

Username: _____

Password: _____

Notes: _____

_____

Website: _____

Username: _____

Password: _____

Notes: _____

_____

Website: _____

Username: _____

Password: _____

Notes: _____

_____

Website: _____

Username: _____

Password: _____

Notes: _____

_____

Website: _____

Username: _____

Password: _____

Notes: _____

_____

Website: _____

Username: _____

Password: _____

Notes: _____

_____

Website: _____
Username: _____
Password: _____
Notes:_____
_____

Website: _____
Username: _____
Password: _____
Notes:_____
_____

Website: _____
Username: _____
Password: _____
Notes:_____
_____

Website: _____

Username: _____

Password: _____

Notes: _____

_____

Website: _____

Username: _____

Password: _____

Notes: _____

_____

Website: _____

Username: _____

Password: _____

Notes: _____

_____

Website: _____

Username: _____

Password: _____

Notes: _____

_____

Website: _____

Username: _____

Password: _____

Notes: _____

_____

Website: _____

Username: _____

Password: _____

Notes: _____

_____

Website: _____

Username: _____

Password: _____

Notes: _____

_____

Website: _____

Username: _____

Password: _____

Notes: _____

_____

Website: _____

Username: _____

Password: _____

Notes: _____

_____

Website: _____

Username: _____

Password: _____

Notes: _____

_____

Website: _____

Username: _____

Password: _____

Notes: _____

_____

Website: _____

Username: _____

Password: _____

Notes: _____

_____

P

Website: _____

Username: _____

Password: _____

Notes:_____

_____

Website: _____

Username: _____

Password: _____

Notes:_____

_____

Website: _____

Username: _____

Password: _____

Notes:_____

_____

Website: _____
Username: _____
Password: _____
Notes: _____

_____

Website: _____
Username: _____
Password: _____
Notes: _____

_____

Website: _____
Username: _____
Password: _____
Notes: _____

_____

P

Website: _____

Username: _____

Password: _____

Notes: _____

_____

Website: _____

Username: _____

Password: _____

Notes: _____

_____

Website: _____

Username: _____

Password: _____

Notes: _____

_____

Website: _____

Username: _____

Password: _____

Notes: _____

_____

Website: _____

Username: _____

Password: _____

Notes: _____

_____

Website: _____

Username: _____

Password: _____

Notes: _____

_____

Website: _____

Username: _____

Password: _____

Notes: _____

_____

Website: _____

Username: _____

Password: _____

Notes: _____

_____

Website: _____

Username: _____

Password: _____

Notes: _____

_____

Website: _____

Username: _____

Password: _____

Notes: _____

_____

Website: _____

Username: _____

Password: _____

Notes: _____

_____

Website: _____

Username: _____

Password: _____

Notes: _____

_____

Website: _____
Username: _____
Password: _____
Notes: _____

_____

Website: _____
Username: _____
Password: _____
Notes: _____

_____

Website: _____
Username: _____
Password: _____
Notes: _____

_____

Website: _____

Username: _____

Password: _____

Notes: _____

_____

Website: _____

Username: _____

Password: _____

Notes: _____

_____

Website: _____

Username: _____

Password: _____

Notes: _____

_____

Website: _____

Username: _____

Password: _____

Notes: _____

_____

Website: _____

Username: _____

Password: _____

Notes: _____

_____

Website: _____

Username: _____

Password: _____

Notes: _____

_____

Website: _____

Username: _____

Password: _____

Notes: _____

_____

Website: _____

Username: _____

Password: _____

Notes: _____

_____

Website: _____

Username: _____

Password: _____

Notes: _____

_____

Website: _____

Username: _____

Password: _____

Notes: _____

_____

Website: _____

Username: _____

Password: _____

Notes: _____

_____

Website: _____

Username: _____

Password: _____

Notes: _____

_____

Website: _____

Username: _____

Password: _____

Notes: _____

_____

Website: _____

Username: _____

Password: _____

Notes: _____

_____

Website: _____

Username: _____

Password: _____

Notes: _____

_____

S

Website: _____

Username: _____

Password: _____

Notes: _____

_____

Website: _____

Username: _____

Password: _____

Notes: _____

_____

Website: _____

Username: _____

Password: _____

Notes: _____

_____

Website: _____
Username: _____
Password: _____
Notes: _____
_____

Website: _____
Username: _____
Password: _____
Notes: _____
_____

Website: _____
Username: _____
Password: _____
Notes: _____
_____

Website: _____

Username: _____

Password: _____

Notes: _____

_____

Website: _____

Username: _____

Password: _____

Notes: _____

_____

Website: _____

Username: _____

Password: _____

Notes: _____

_____

Website: _____

Username: _____

Password: _____

Notes: _____

_____

Website: _____

Username: _____

Password: _____

Notes: _____

_____

Website: _____

Username: _____

Password: _____

Notes: _____

_____

Website: _____
Username: _____
Password: _____
Notes:_____
_____

Website: _____
Username: _____
Password: _____
Notes:_____
_____

Website: _____
Username: _____
Password: _____
Notes:_____
_____

Website: _____
Username: _____
Password: _____
Notes: _____
_____

Website: _____
Username: _____
Password: _____
Notes: _____
_____

Website: _____
Username: _____
Password: _____
Notes: _____
_____

Website: _____

Username: _____

Password: _____

Notes: _____

_____

Website: _____

Username: _____

Password: _____

Notes: _____

_____

Website: _____

Username: _____

Password: _____

Notes: _____

_____

Website: _____

Username: _____

Password: _____

Notes: _____

_____

Website: _____

Username: _____

Password: _____

Notes: _____

_____

Website: _____

Username: _____

Password: _____

Notes: _____

_____

Website: _____

Username: _____

Password: _____

Notes: _____

_____

Website: _____

Username: _____

Password: _____

Notes: _____

_____

Website: _____

Username: _____

Password: _____

Notes: _____

_____

Website: _____

Username: _____

Password: _____

Notes: _____

_____

Website: _____

Username: _____

Password: _____

Notes: _____

_____

Website: _____

Username: _____

Password: _____

Notes: _____

_____

Website: _____

Username: _____

Password: _____

Notes: _____

_____

Website: _____

Username: _____

Password: _____

Notes: _____

_____

Website: _____

Username: _____

Password: _____

Notes: _____

_____

Website: _____
Username: _____
Password: _____
Notes:_____

_____

Website: _____
Username: _____
Password: _____
Notes:_____

_____

Website: _____
Username: _____
Password: _____
Notes:_____

_____

Website: _____

Username: _____

Password: _____

Notes: _____

_____

Website: _____

Username: _____

Password: _____

Notes: _____

_____

Website: _____

Username: _____

Password: _____

Notes: _____

_____

Website: _____
Username: _____
Password: _____
Notes:_____

_____

Website: _____
Username: _____
Password: _____
Notes:_____

_____

Website: _____
Username: _____
Password: _____
Notes:_____

_____

Website: _____

Username: _____

Password: _____

Notes: _____

_____

Website: _____

Username: _____

Password: _____

Notes: _____

_____

Website: _____

Username: _____

Password: _____

Notes: _____

_____

Website: _____

Username: _____

Password: _____

Notes: _____

_____

Website: _____

Username: _____

Password: _____

Notes: _____

_____

Website: _____

Username: _____

Password: _____

Notes: _____

_____

Website: _____

Username: _____

Password: _____

Notes: _____

_____

Website: _____

Username: _____

Password: _____

Notes: _____

_____

Website: _____

Username: _____

Password: _____

Notes: _____

_____

Website: _____

Username: _____

Password: _____

Notes: _____

_____

Website: _____

Username: _____

Password: _____

Notes: _____

_____

Website: _____

Username: _____

Password: _____

Notes: _____

_____

Website: _____

Username: _____

Password: _____

Notes: _____

_____

Website: _____

Username: _____

Password: _____

Notes: _____

_____

Website: _____

Username: _____

Password: _____

Notes: _____

_____

Website: _____

Username: _____

Password: _____

Notes: _____

_____

Website: _____

Username: _____

Password: _____

Notes: _____

_____

Website: _____

Username: _____

Password: _____

Notes: _____

_____

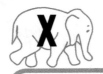

X

Website: _____

Username: _____

Password: _____

Notes: _____

_____

Website: _____

Username: _____

Password: _____

Notes: _____

_____

Website: _____

Username: _____

Password: _____

Notes: _____

_____

Website: _____

Username: _____

Password: _____

Notes: _____

_____

Website: _____

Username: _____

Password: _____

Notes: _____

_____

Website: _____

Username: _____

Password: _____

Notes: _____

_____

Website: _____

Username: _____

Password: _____

Notes: _____

_____

Website: _____

Username: _____

Password: _____

Notes: _____

_____

Website: _____

Username: _____

Password: _____

Notes: _____

_____

Website: _____
Username: _____
Password: _____
Notes:_____
_____

Website: _____
Username: _____
Password: _____
Notes:_____
_____

Website: _____
Username: _____
Password: _____
Notes:_____
_____

Website: _____

Username: _____

Password: _____

Notes: _____

_____

Website: _____

Username: _____

Password: _____

Notes: _____

_____

Website: _____

Username: _____

Password: _____

Notes: _____

_____

www.ingramcontent.com/pod-product-compliance
Lightning Source LLC
Chambersburg PA
CBHW071301050326
40690CB00011B/2486